GET INTO YOGA

JAIME WINTERS

CRABTREE
Publishing Company
www.crabtreebooks.com

Author: Jaime Winters

Publishing plan research and development: Reagan Miller

Editors: Marcia Abramson, Petrice Custance

Photo research: Melissa McClellan

Editorial director: Kathy Middleton

Proofreader: Wendy Scavuzzo

Cover/interior design: T.J. Choleva

Production coordinator and prepress technician: Samara Parent

Print coordinator: Margaret Amy Salter

Consultant: Sandee Ewasiuk
Certified Yoga Instructor

Written and produced for Crabtree Publishing
by BlueApple*Works* Inc.

Photographs

Shutterstock.com: © Photo_mts (cover background); © Romolo Tavani (cover center background); © naluwan (cover center left); © kryzhov (cover center right); © vasanty (cover bottom left); © Levranii (cover far left); © alexkatkov (TOC background, p. 10 top); © Sokolova23 (TOC bottom left); © iofoto (p. 5 top right); © wavebreakmedia (p. 5 bottom); © Photographee.eu (p. 6 top); © NEstudio (p. 6 bottom); © Anna Moskvina (p. 7 top left); © coka (p. 7 top right); © Dojo666 (p. 7 left); © Rob Marmion (p. 8, 14); © Anna Hoychuk (p. 11 middle); © VGstockstudio (p. 11 bottom); © Mangostar (p. 15 bottom);

istockphoto © Joseph C. Justice Jr. (cover top left)

© Sam Taylor: cover, back cover, TP, TOC, p. 4, 9, 10 bottom, 11 top, 12, 13, 15 top, 16–31

Library and Archives Canada Cataloguing in Publication

Winters, Jaime, author
      Get into yoga / Jaime Winters.

(Get-into-it guides)
Includes index.
Issued in print and electronic formats.
ISBN 978-0-7787-3644-8 (hardcover).--
ISBN 978-0-7787-3653-0 (softcover).--
ISBN 978-1-4271-1964-3 (HTML)

      1. Yoga--Health aspects--Juvenile literature. 2. Yoga--Juvenile
literature. 3. Stress management for children--Juvenile literature.
I. Title.

RA781.67.W56 2017   j613.7'046   C2017-903619-X
                                              C2017-903620-3

Library of Congress Cataloging-in-Publication Data

CIP available at the Library of Congress

Crabtree Publishing Company
www.crabtreebooks.com   1-800-387-7650

Printed in Canada/092017/PB20170719

Published in Canada
Crabtree Publishing
616 Welland Ave.
St. Catharines, Ontario
L2M 5V6

Published in the United States
Crabtree Publishing
PMB 59051
350 Fifth Avenue, 59th Floor
New York, New York 10118

Published in the United Kingdom
Crabtree Publishing
Maritime House
Basin Road North, Hove
BN41 1WR

Published in Australia
Crabtree Publishing
3 Charles Street
Coburg North
VIC, 3058

CONTENTS

YOGA THROUGH TIME

Yoga is not like any other type of exercise. First of all, yoga isn't only about exercise. The practice of yoga also encourages proper nutrition, relaxation, and positive thinking. Yoga is about being healthy and balanced in both your body and your mind.

ANCIENT ORIGINS

No one knows when people first took up yoga. Some say it started at the dawn of human civilization. But clay seals made nearly 5,000 years ago, in what is now India, show people sitting with their feet tucked under their buttocks just like modern **yogis** and **yoginis**. The word "yoga" means to unite the mind, body, and spirit. It comes from the ancient **Sanskrit** word *yuj* for "join" or "unite." Sanskrit is the language that ancient **gurus** used to teach yoga. Many gurus, teachers, and students still call yoga poses by their Sanskrit names today. About 2,000 years ago, a **sage** named Patanjali wrote down the oral teachings of yoga in the Yoga Sutras. In the Middle Ages, the years from 500 to 1500, different types of yoga arose based on living a spiritual life. Around 700, people began to combine body poses, breathing, and **meditation** into a practice a lot like modern yoga.

June 21 is International Yoga Day. Just as yoga unites the mind, body, and spirit, the annual celebration encourages people to see themselves as one with the world and nature.

Yoga in the West

Yoga didn't begin to catch on in North America until the 1890s, when gurus, such as Swami Vivekananda, began to arrive. But they focused on breathing and meditation, not **asanas**—the physical poses. It wasn't until 1947, when Indra Devi opened a yoga studio in Hollywood and taught the poses to movie stars, that it began to take off. Devi was the first woman to study yoga with Indian guru Tirumalai Krishnamacharya. At first, the guru said it was impossible for him to teach her, because yoga was for Indian men only. But when she would not give up, he agreed. Devi developed a yoga style that grew into the yoga that millions of North Americans practice today. Two other students of Krishnamacharya, B.K.S. Iyengar and Pattabhi Jois, also developed popular types of yoga.

How to Use This Book

The poses in this book are easy enough for you to try at home. A yoga class at school or in a yoga studio is a great way to learn more. This book will give you a great introduction to the world of yoga.

Bring Your Mat to Class

Not only to gym, but to math, science, and art. Schools include yoga in a variety of classes to help kids develop tools to bust stress, focus energy, manage anger, communicate, improve sports performance, and stay mentally healthy.

WHAT'S YOUR TYPE?

So you want to get into yoga. What type would be the best for you? Check out these four popular types of yoga and see.

Hatha yoga is great for beginners. It includes many breathing exercises.

HATHA YOGA

No matter what type of yoga you get into, it's hatha yoga. In Sanskrit, *hatha* means "force" or "effort." Today, the term "hatha yoga" refers to the physical poses of yoga. All types of yoga in North America are hatha yoga. However, "hatha yoga" has also come to mean a gentle type of yoga centered around the most basic poses. Do a hatha yoga class and you're likely to leave feeling more relaxed, longer, and looser without having worked up a sweat. What's more, hatha yoga is great for beginning yogis and yoginis.

ASHTANGA YOGA

Want to get physical and heat things up? Try **Ashtanga yoga**. You'll flow through a vigorous sequence of standing poses, balance poses, seated poses, twists, and backbends. And you'll move with your breath. In fact, every move you make in Ashtanga is linked to an inhale or exhale of breath. Each pose has a movement linked to breath that connects it to the next pose. Linking breath and movement like this connects the mind and body together and produces heat. This makes you sweat, purifying the body. Named after the Sanskrit word for "eight limbs," Ashtanga yoga has eight stages. But according to Pattabhi Jois, the late guru of Ashtanga, everyone starts with the third one—asana.

A yoga teacher may guide students into proper form.

IYENGAR YOGA

It won't make you jump to the moon and back or raise your heart rate, but **Iyengar yoga** will still challenge you. The late B.K.S. Iyengar believed that properly positioning the body in each pose is the most important thing in yoga. He had students focus on details of the body to find the correct alignment in each pose. He encouraged students to pay close attention to how their body was feeling during each pose to find the proper position for their individual body. Students were able to use items such as bands or blocks to help them achieve their proper position. Iyengar also had students hold each pose for a long time to develop strength, flexibility, and awareness, and to bring the mind, body, and spirit into balance.

Iyengar yoga uses bands, blocks, and other props to get the body into proper position.

Vinyasa is a good class to take after you learn the poses in beginning yoga.

VINYASA YOGA

If you like to move to the groove, rock out in a **Vinyasa yoga** class. No joke! You'll flow through moves as if dancing, from one pose to the next, to the beat of lively music. Vinyasa yoga comes from Ashtanga yoga. So each movement is linked to the breath. However, unlike Ashtanga, Vinyasa yoga does not follow a set sequence of poses. Teachers choreograph their classes, stringing poses together to challenge and inspire students and to change things up. You'll find that no two teachers or classes are the same. So if routine bores you to tears, give Vinyasa yoga a whirl.

Did You Know?

The eight limbs of Ashtanga are: yama, or moral codes; niyama, or self-purification or study; asanas, or poses; pranayama, or breath control; pratyahara, or sense control; dharana, or concentration; dhyana, or meditation; and samadhi, or contemplation.

Some Like It Hot

Get set to sweat buckets in a **Bikram** or hot yoga class. Not only is the heat cranked up high in the studio, but students also shimmy through a set list of 26 vigorous poses. Chances are you might find it too hot to handle until you hit your teens.

BENEFITS OF YOGA

You don't have to be a genius or a yoga guru to know that this ancient practice is good for you. (Why else pick up this book and do it, right?) But that doesn't mean that knowing a little bit about the benefits can't take you a long way, fire you up to do it, and even help you stick with it.

SOMETHING TO TWIST AND SHOUT ABOUT

Many people believe practicing yoga is life changing. Yoga helps to relax tense muscles and energize the body. Yoga also helps many people develop a better understanding of themselves and the world around them. How does yoga do this? Yoga requires deep and focused breathing during each pose, which helps quiet your mind, clear your thoughts, and release stress, allowing your mind to rest. This helps many people feel an inner calm, which also helps them feel more confident. Over time, this calmness and confidence can be brought into everyday life. Thanks to yoga, some people find themselves able to deal with stressful situations that they never thought they could handle. Yoga helps to strengthen the mind as well as the body.

Did You Know?

When the **Dalai Lama** said the following in 2012, it went **viral**: "If every 8-year-old in the world is taught meditation, we will eliminate violence from the world within one generation."

FLOW WITH THE BREATH

Ever noticed how your body goes with the flow of your breath? For example, as you inhale, your body tends to open or expand. And as you exhale, your body tends to close or fold up. The same holds true in yoga. Try to lift or move into poses as you inhale, and fold or exit poses as you exhale. Take five deep breaths in each pose. And on each exhale, see if you can move a bit deeper into the pose.

THE SEVEN CHAKRAS

A rainbow of colors symbolize the seven **chakras** of the human spine. *Chakra* means "wheel" or "ring" in Sanskrit, and each one is like a coil of energy. The *chakras* are connected to different emotional, spiritual, and physical states. These energy centers reflect our thoughts, feelings, and experiences and, if they get blocked, injury or illness may result. Practicing yoga is a way of uncoiling their energy.

Sahasrara, the crown chakra, connects to **mindfulness** *and understanding.*

Anahata, the heart chakra, connects to love and **compassion***.*

Ajna, the brow chakra, connects to **intuition** *and* **instinct***.*

Manipura, the chakra in the pit of the stomach, connects to confidence and personal power.

Vishuddha, the throat chakra, connects to communication and expressing ourselves.

Svadhisthana, the chakra along the spine above the belly button, connects to emotions and creativity.

Muladhara, the root chakra at the base of the spine, connects to safety and survival.

SWAMIJI'S FIVE POINTS OF YOGA

Swamiji Vishnudevananda didn't know the meaning of impossible. In 1932, when he was a five-year-old in India, he wanted to go to school. "Impossible," everyone said. "The nearest school is more than five miles away." The next day, he rose early, packed a lunch, and hiked through the jungle to school. After that, young Vishnudevananda went to school every day. When he grew up, he studied **Sivananda yoga** and became a great teacher known as Swamiji. He summed it up into the following five simple points that make it easy for people to practice daily.

1. PROPER EXERCISE

We are born to move. If our bodies don't get physical exercise, eventually disease and discomfort set in. "Proper exercise" should feel good and benefit the mind, body, and spirit. Practicing yoga does this. It develops strength and flexibility in the spine, which holds the nervous system.

2. PROPER BREATHING

Breath is vital energy, or **prana**. When we can control the breath, we can control the mind. By practicing yoga, we can learn to control the breath. Proper breathing is deep, slow, and steady, and it can increase energy and help the mind see things clearly.

MINDFULNESS

Get Into It

Can you catch your mind when it monkeys around? Try to notice when your mind jumps out of the present moment into the past or future. Then bring your attention to your breath to bring it back to the here and now.

Have you ever arrived at your best friend's on your bike only to realize that you don't remember a thing about the ride over? You're not alone. Most people have "monkey mind" moments like this, when their mind jumps around from the present event to those in the past and future. Mindfulness is a way to be present by focusing your attention on where you are and what you are doing. You can be mindful by paying attention to the sights and sounds around you, as well as any physical sensations that come up.

3. PROPER RELAXATION

Life in the modern world makes it difficult to relax. But relaxation is essential, because it's our body's natural way of recharging. Our body and mind can't perform well without it. Yoga helps people relax physically, mentally, and spiritually, calming tensions and emotions, so we can recharge our "batteries."

4. PROPER DIET

We eat to give ourselves prana, the vital energy of life. The foods we eat not only nourish our body, but also affect our mind. A healthy diet of fresh, simple foods that are easily digested provides the best fuel for yogis and yoginis. Avoiding substances that can overstimulate the brain, such as caffeine, can help calm the mind and sharpen the intellect.

5. POSITIVE THINKING AND MEDITATION

Whatever we think, we become. So, to be happy and healthy, we need to think positive thoughts. We can develop positive thoughts by practicing yoga and meditation. Regular meditation develops our ability to control our mind, which leads to peace of mind. Meditation also helps our physical health by strengthening the **immune system**. Is it any wonder Swamiji considered this as the most important point of all?

MANTRAS

Mantras are sounds, words, or phrases that you can sing or chant over and over to reprogram that monkey mind of yours from negative worries to positive thoughts. A popular mantra is *om* (pronounced "awm"), the Sanskrit word for the "sound of the universe." Another is *so ham* (pronounced "so hum"), which means "I am that—the universal self." Yet another is "May I be happy." Traditionally, gurus gave mantras to their students. Today, in North America, yogis and yoginis often choose their own mantras. What will your mantra be?

THREE-PART BREATH

Feeling nervous? Want to calm your mind? Breathe deeply into your belly, chest, and throat like this:

1. Get comfortable by sitting with your legs crossed or by lying on your back with bent knees.

2. Place one hand on your belly and the other on your chest.

3. Close your mouth to breathe in and out through your nose only.

4. Exhale all your air through your nose.

5. Keep inhaling into your chest to fill your lungs.

6. Keep inhaling into your throat. When your throat is full, hold your breath for a few seconds.

7. Now go backward, slowly breathing out all the air, first through the throat, then the chest, then the belly. Can you feel your chest and belly sink as you exhale?

8. Repeat steps 4 to 7 five to 10 times. How do you feel now?

Without even thinking about it, you take 20,000 to 30,000 breaths a day. But do you breathe deeply? Your breath often reflects what you're feeling or thinking. When you're frustrated, you might huff and puff. When you're tired, you might sigh, and when you're scared, you might get short of breath or even hold your breath. No wonder breathing is part of yoga. When you notice how you breathe, you can change it. And by changing how you breathe, you can change how you feel. For example, by taking long deep breaths, we can feel calm. By taking a bunch of short, sharp breaths, we can feel more energetic. Check out some of these yogic breathing techniques.

SEAL IT WITH A MUDRA

Mudras are hand poses. In Sanskrit, *mudra* means "seal." You can do a mudra during a breathing exercise to seal in the energy of the breath, or anytime you want to shift energy from how you feel to how you want to feel. Sit cross-legged with your eyes closed and try your hand at these.

Rest the back of your hands on your knees and bring the tips of your index fingers under the tips of your thumbs. Extend your other fingers so they are straight but relaxed. This pose is called wisdom seal, or jnana mudra.

Hold up your right hand with your palm facing forward and your fingers together. Rest your left hand on your left thigh. Your right hand symbolizes peace and fearlessness.

LEFT, RIGHT: ALTERNATE NOSTRIL BREATHING

Breathing through one nostril at a time leads to an even breath, even mind, and can even put your feelings on an even keel.

1 *Do wisdom seal with your left hand.*

2 *With your right hand, place your index and middle fingers on your forehead between your eyebrows. Bring your thumb to the right side of your nose and your ring and pinky fingers to the left side.*

3 *Close the right nostril by pressing your thumb against it and breathe in through the left. Close the left nostril by pressing your ring and pinky fingers against it.*

4 *Open the right nostril and breathe out. Then breathe in and close the right nostril. Open the left nostril, breathe out, then breathe in and repeat. Do a number of rounds.*

Get Into It!

Once you're comfortable doing alternate nostril breathing, try to lengthen your exhales to become twice as long as your inhales.

LION'S BREATH

Need to chase away stress, blow off steam, or lighten up?
Roar like a lion.

1 *Sit cross-legged with your hands on your knees. Lift your chest to sit up tall and open your heart.*

2 *Do wisdom seal with both hands. Close your mouth and inhale through the nose.*

3 *Open your mouth wide, stick out your tongue toward your chin, and slowly exhale, roaring "Aaaah!"*

4 *Close your mouth to breathe in. Then roar again for as many times as you want to vent any excess stress, frustration, or worry.*

GETTING STARTED

Mind. Body. Breath. You don't need much else to do yoga. Most people do like to use a mat that can be rolled out on the floor to create a non-slippery spot to practice on. Many stores and websites sell yoga mats. If you don't have a mat, put down a big towel on carpet. Just make sure your yoga spot is not slippery. After trying yoga at home, taking classes with an experienced teacher is a way to build on what you learn in this book. Ask your family to check out yoga classes for kids at your local school, recreation center, or yoga studio. Slip into some comfortable exercise clothes and try out a class.

BEND AND TWIST

Can you bend forward, backward, and to the side? Can you twist, too? Awesome. Now can you name the part of your body that all these moves hinge on and revolve around? If you said your spine, you're right. Many yoga poses call upon the spine to move in one of these four basic ways. Check these out:

Did You Know?

Early birds rule the mat! According to researchers, we're more likely to start and finish a yoga practice if we do it in the morning.

Forward Bend

Sanskrit Name: Paschimottanasana, which means "intense west stretch"

Benefits: Quiets the brain, reduces stress, stretches the spine, shoulders, and hamstrings, aids digestion, relieves headaches

Make It Your Own: Don't worry if you can't grab your feet with straight legs yet. Just bend your knees. You might also put a pillow under your bent knees for support.

Cobra Backbend

Sanskrit Name: Bhujangasana, which means "snake pose"

Benefits: Strengthens the spine, sparks digestion, stretches the belly, chest, and shoulders

Make It Your Own: If this feels too intense or your shoulders are tight, don't lift the chest as high. Allow your elbows to bend more.

Side Bend

Sanskrit Name: Parsva Tadasana,
which means "side mountain pose "

Benefits: Tones the muscles along
the sides of the belly, ribs, and spine,
and allows for full breathing

Make It Your Own:
If this is challenging,
ease up from the bend
a bit and breathe
into the area
where you feel
the stretch.

Tip

Pain doesn't equal gain.
If moving into or holding a
pose hurts, ease up. Back off to
a position you can hold without
pain. Or ask your teacher to
help you modify the pose
so you feel no pain.

Twisted Easy Pose

Sanskrit Name: Parivrtta Sukhasana, which means
"revolved easy pose"

Benefits: Stretches the hips, knees, and ankles, improves
flexibility in the spine, chest, and shoulders, reduces
stress, boosts energy, and help kidneys and digestive
tract do their jobs

Make It Your Own: If it's tough to sit upright in this pose,
sit on blankets or a pillow so your hips are as high as
your knees.

GREETINGS FROM THE MAT

Namaste! There's no better way to show respect
and gratitude than this ancient Sanskrit greeting.
At the beginning and end of class, teacher and
student often say *namaste* to each other, placing
their hands together at the heart chakra and bowing
their heads. While *nama* means "bow" and *te* means
"you," the English translation is "I bow to you."
The greeting is a way of saying "the spirit within
me salutes the spirit in you."

SEATED POSES

Not only do seated poses bring you close to the ground, but they can also bring you and your busy brain down to earth. What's more, they're perfect for beginners starting any yoga practice and meditating.

EASY POSE (SUKHASANA)

Ease into some seated poses with this steady and comfortable pose—and smile. *Sukha* is Sanskrit for joy or pleasure. Even though holding Easy Pose might not feel like work, it increases flexibility in the hips and spine and prepares you to take on more advanced poses.

Get Into It!

Make Easy Pose your go-to for breathing exercises or meditation. Set a timer to breathe or meditate for five minutes. Over time, increase this amount of time and see how long you can breathe or meditate in the pose.

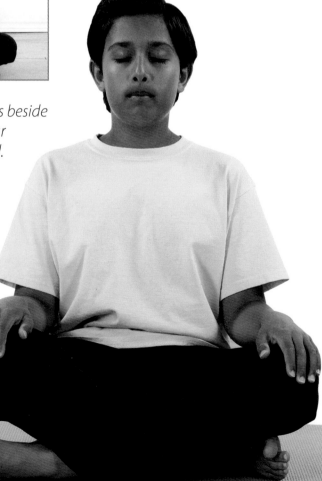

1 *Sit on the floor. Cross your legs so your left shin is on top of your right shin.*

2 *Place your palms beside your hips, so your fingers point backward. Press into your palms and slide your feet toward the knees.*

4 *Keeping the length you found in your spine, rest your palms on your knees. Take five deep breaths.*

3 *Press into the palms to lift the chest and lengthen the spine.*

HERO POSE (VIRASANA)

Hero Pose can strengthen your legs, help you digest food, and even help you pass gas.

Tip

If your ankles, knees, or shins feel crushed against your mat in Hero Pose, put a blanket on top of your mat to cushion them.

1 *Kneel on your mat. Bring your knees together and sit on your heels. If this pains or strains your knees, sit on a stack of blankets instead to raise your hips.*

2 *Rest your palms on your thighs. Lift your chest to lengthen your spine. Take five deep breaths.*

HALF LOTUS POSE (ARDHA PADMASANA)

Easy Pose and Hero Pose help prepare for half lotus. But don't worry if it takes a while to get the hang of it. Some people can do Half Lotus on the first try. Others need time for their hips to become flexible enough. So just breathe and let your lotus bloom in its own time.

1 *Move into Easy Pose (at left).*

2 *Use your hands to lift your right leg and foot.*

3 *Place the top of the right foot on the left thigh in front of the hip. Sit up straight.*

4 *Rest the back of your hands on your knees. Bring the tips of your index fingers and thumbs together, and extend the other fingers in jnana mudra (see page 12). Take five deep breaths. Repeat the steps with the left leg on top.*

STANDING POSES

Standing tall in these poses will wake up your arms and legs, open your hips, and energize your entire spine. That's not all. Standing poses will center you within yourself, so you can feel strong and confident.

Tip

In Mountain Pose, imagine that your ears, shoulders, hips, knees, and ankles are all lined up like pieces of Lego stacked one on top of the other.

MOUNTAIN POSE (TADASANA)

Stand tall and firm like a mountain to connect to the earth beneath your feet and feel your own inner strength and power.

1 *Stand with your feet together, big toes touching, and heels slightly apart. Have your arms at your sides.*

2 *Let your shoulders fall away from your ears, and your shoulder blades melt down your back.*

3 *Press the soles of your feet firmly into the ground. Lift your chest and the top of your head toward the sky.*

4 *Look straight ahead and take five deep breaths.*

Step into a pose of power and strength that will boost your stamina and improve your balance.

1 Stand tall in Mountain Pose as at left. Bring your hands together at your chest.

2 With your right foot, take a big step to the right, so your feet are one leg length apart.

3 Raise your arms out to the sides in line with your shoulders. Turn your right foot **parallel** to the edge of your mat, and turn your left toes slightly in.

4 Bend your right knee, so it hovers above your ankle. Turn your head to the right and look over your right fingertips. Hold the pose for five deep breaths.

5 Reverse the steps to release the pose then do Warrior II on the left side.

19

What does it take to sit without a chair, stand tall like a tree, or stand on one leg like a stork? Strength and balance. Try these poses and see.

Get Into It!

The longer you hold Chair Pose, the more strength you'll build. Set a timer and challenge yourself. Can you hold it for 30 seconds? One minute?

1

Stand in Mountain Pose.

Inhale and raise your arms overhead with your palms facing each other.

2

3

4

5

CHAIR POSE (UTKATASANA)

Hold this pose and you may look like you're sitting in an invisible chair, but you won't feel that way. You might even feel a little wobbly. Not only does the pose demand strength, but it builds strength in the legs and spine. Is it any wonder its Sanskrit name means "fierce pose"?

Exhale and bend your knees. Slowly lower your buttocks as though you were sitting down in a chair. Bring your thighs as parallel to the floor as you can.

Lift your chest toward your hands and press your palms together. Hold the pose for five deep breaths. On each exhale, try to sit a little lower.

To come out of the pose, inhale and straighten your legs.

TREE POSE (VRKSASANA)

Think you can stand on one leg and breathe at the same time? Try it and see. This pose will improve your balance and power of concentration.

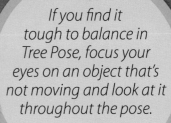

Tip

If you find it tough to balance in Tree Pose, focus your eyes on an object that's not moving and look at it throughout the pose.

1

Stand in Mountain Pose.

2

Shift your weight onto the left foot. On an inhale, lift your right foot, grab your shin, and pull the right foot to your left inner thigh or calf.

3

Place the sole of the right foot on the left thigh. Press the foot and the thigh together. Bring your hands together in front of your chest.

4

Keep pressing the foot and thigh together. Raise your hands above your head. Take five deep breaths.

5

On an exhale, lower your hands back in front of your chest and slide the right foot down and release it. Then repeat the steps with the left foot.

Get Into It!

Can you keep your balance in Tree Pose as you press your palms together and raise them above your head? How about with your eyes closed?

STORK POSE (BAKASANA)

If you think it's for the birds, think again. Stork Pose will help you develop balance and coordination.

❶ *Stand in Mountain Pose and bring your hands together in front of your chest.*

❷ *Press firmly into the soles of your feet and lift the top of your head toward the sky.*

❸ *Shift weight onto your left foot. Slowly raise your right leg until your right thigh is parallel with the floor. Keep your right toes pointed toward the floor.*

❹ *If you feel steady, inhale and stretch your arms out. Hold the pose for five breaths.*

❺ *On an exhale, lower your right leg to the floor. Repeat the steps with your left leg.*

GROUNDING POSES

You're grounded! Check out some standing poses that give "getting grounded" a whole new meaning. Not only will they give you a chance to feel connected to the earth, but they'll also let you play with gravity.

Tip

In Downward Dog Pose, your head is lower than your heart. This allows fresh blood to flow to your brain, which can recharge your "batteries" if you feel tired.

DOWNWARD DOG POSE (ADHO MUKHA SHVANASANA)

Have you ever seen a dog stretch by lifting its butt high in the air? This pose is named after that playful canine move. In Sanskrit, *adho mukha* means "downward facing" and *shvan* means "dog." Get down on all fours and check it out.

Get onto your hands and knees with a straight back. Bring your shoulders above your wrists and your hips above your knees.

Curl your toes under.

Inhale. As you exhale, lift your knees, straightening your legs and raising your hips toward the sky. Let your head drop toward the earth, bringing your ears beside your arms.

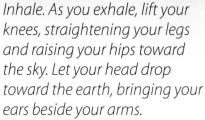

Press your heels toward the floor. Feel your feet and palms grounding you on the earth. Take five deep breaths.

Exhale and bend your knees to release the pose and move into Child's Pose (see page 26) for five deep breaths.

TRIANGLE POSE (UTTHITA TRIKONASANA)

Can you spot two triangles that the yogini shown in this pose is making with her body?

1 Stand in Mountain Pose.

2 Exhale and turn to the right, stepping out with your right foot so your feet are one leg length apart. Turn your right foot parallel to the edge of your mat and turn your left toes slightly in.

3 Inhale and raise your arms out to the sides in line with your shoulders, palms facing down.

4 As you exhale, reach forward with your right arm. Bring your right hand down to rest on your ankle or shin (use a block if you can't reach) and extend your left arm up.

5 Turn your head to look at your left hand. Hold the pose for five deep breaths. Repeat the steps to do Triangle Pose on the left side.

23

TWISTING POSES

What does your spine have in common with a wet sponge mop? It needs to be wrung out! And twists are the perfect pose for the job. Your spine has spongy discs that absorb blood and waste. When you twist, you help squeeze out the old blood and waste, so the discs can absorb fresh blood. Twists also massage your inner organs such as the kidneys, and fire up your digestive system.

HALF LORD OF THE FISHES POSE (ARDHA MATSYENDRASANA)

Twist and turn into this pose that targets your shoulders, upper back, and arms.

Sit on the floor with your legs out in front of you and your arms at your sides.

Bend both of your knees so that the soles of your feet are flat on the floor.

Lower your left knee to the floor. Put your left foot under your right leg so that your foot is next to your right buttock.

While inhaling, lift your left arm above your head.

While exhaling, twist to the right. Put your left elbow on the outside of your right knee.

Turn your head so you are looking straight ahead. Stay in this position for up to a minute. Repeat the steps on the other side.

SUPINE SPINAL TWIST POSE (SUPTA MATSYENDRASANA)

Chill out with a twist for your lower back that will help you be calm and keep going.

1 *Lie **supine** (on your back) and hug your knees to your chest.*

2 *Clasp your left hand around your right knee. Straighten your left leg and bring it to the floor.*

3 *Extend your right arm out to the side, palm facing up.*

4 *With your left hand, draw your right knee to the left as you twist through the spine.*

5 *Turn your head to the right to look at your right palm. Take five deep breaths. Exhale to unwind. Repeat the steps to twist to the opposite side.*

When you want to unwind, hang loose, or just chill, nothing beats yoga. Stress relief and relaxation are two of its top benefits. In fact, many yoga classes start and finish with poses to relax both mind and body.

CHILD'S POSE (BALASANA)

Any time you need a break in yoga, go into Child's Pose. Not only will it calm your mind, but it will also relieve stress and stretch your hips, thighs, and back.

Kneel and sit on your heels.

Lean forward and place your hands in front of you on the mat.

Fold forward, resting your chest on your thighs and your forehead on the mat.

 Exhale. Release the pose and inhale to sit up.

KNEES-TO-CHEST POSE (APANASANA)

Try this pose and give yourself a big hug.

Lie on your back.

1

Bend your knees and hug them to your chest. Take five deep breaths.

2

To massage your back, gently rock your knees from side to side.

3

CORPSE POSE (SAVASANA)

Don't worry about meeting zombies in this pose. Just let your concerns melt into nothing and "come back from the dead" totally refreshed.

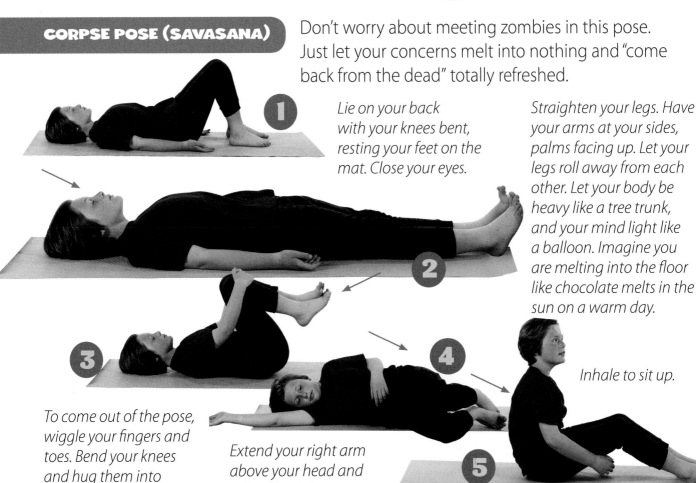

1

Lie on your back with your knees bent, resting your feet on the mat. Close your eyes.

Straighten your legs. Have your arms at your sides, palms facing up. Let your legs roll away from each other. Let your body be heavy like a tree trunk, and your mind light like a balloon. Imagine you are melting into the floor like chocolate melts in the sun on a warm day.

2

3

4

Inhale to sit up.

To come out of the pose, wiggle your fingers and toes. Bend your knees and hug them into your chest.

Extend your right arm above your head and roll to the right.

5

SALUTE THE SUN

What's a surefire way to wake up, cheer up, and boost your energy? Roll through a few sun salutations. Many people start their day with this ancient sequence of forward bends and backbends.

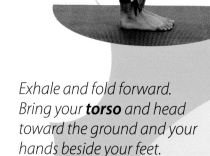

(2) *Inhale and reach up. Bring your hands together above your head and look up at your thumbs.*

(3) *Exhale and fold forward. Bring your **torso** and head toward the ground and your hands beside your feet.*

(1) *Stand tall in Mountain Pose with your feet together, big toes touching, and heels slightly apart. Exhale.*

108 or Bust

*The number 108 is sacred in yoga and in several Eastern religions, including Hinduism. It's not known exactly how this belief began, but the distance from Earth to the Sun is about 108 times the **diameter** of the Sun. Today, yogis and yoginis often do 108 sun salutations to mark the changing seasons. By saluting the sun, they give their energy as an offering of peace or unity to the world.*

(12) *Exhale and move back to Mountain Pose. Repeat the steps to do Sun Salutes a few more times.*

(11) *Inhale and reach up, bringing your hands together above your head. Look up.*

(10) *Exhale and fold forward. Bring your torso and head toward the ground and your hands beside your feet.*

Inhale and bend your right leg while extending your left foot back into a lunge position.

4

Exhale and step or jump your right foot back. Slowly lower into a push-up position, bringing your body parallel to the floor.

5

Lower your body onto the mat. Place your hands so your fingertips are in line with your shoulders and your elbows bent at your sides.

6

Did You Know?

As you did Sun Salute A, did you notice that the steps after Downward Dog Pose mirror the steps at the beginning, but in reverse order? It's a circular pattern, like the Sun itself.

Inhale and press into the palms to lift into Cobra Backbend (see page 14) with your elbows bent or straight arms.

7

Exhale and curl your toes under as you lift your hips into Downward Dog Pose. Press your heels into the floor and take five deep breaths.

8

9

Inhale and jump, or step, your feet to your hands. Look up.

LEARNING MORE

BOOKS

Personal Trainer: Yoga for Kids: The at-home yoga class for young beginners by Liz Lark, Carlton Books, 2011.

Yoga for Beginners: 35 Simple Yoga Poses to Calm Your Mind and Strengthen Your Body by Cory Martin, Althea Press, 2015.

Yoga for you: Feel calmer, stronger, happier! by Rebecca Rissman, Walter Foster Jr, 2017.

WEBSITES

An explanation of different types of yoga, how to get started in yoga, and how to stay on track.
http://kidshealth.org/en/teens/yoga.html

Yoga for stress relief
http://kidshealth.org/en/teens/yoga-stress.html?WT.ac=t-ra#

Yoga, meditation, breathing, and visualization
http://kidshealth.org/en/teens/meditation.html?WT.ac=t-ra

Find a yoga class
www.yogafinder.com

Check out this website for information, tips, and more
www.yogajournal.com

A free guided-meditation smartphone app to download
http://smilingmind.com.au/smiling-mind-app/

Stop, Breathe & Think App
http://www.stopbreathethink.org/

GLOSSARY

asanas (ah-SAH-nahz) Yoga poses

Ashtanga (ash-TANG-ah) **yoga**
A type of yoga in which a series of poses are linked together through breath and movement and practiced in order

Bikram yoga A type of yoga made up of 26 vigorous poses practiced in a hot room

chakra (SHAH-krah) Energy centers within the human body that are connected to different emotional, physical, and spiritual states

compassion Sympathy and concern for others

Dalai Lama The spiritual leader of Tibetan Buddhists

diameter A straight line through the center of a circle or sphere

guru An accomplished teacher or expert

immune system A collection of cells, tissues, and organs that work together to protect the body

instinct The way people or animals naturally react or behave, without having to think or learn about it

intuition An ability to understand or know something immediately based on your feelings rather than facts

Iyengar (eye-YEN-gar) **yoga** A type of yoga developed by the late guru B.K.S. Iyengar that focuses on proper body alignment

mantra Sounds, words, or phrases sung or chanted over and over to reprogram the mind from negative worries to positive thoughts

meditation Action or practice of focusing inward, trying to empty the mind of thoughts and observe the breath

mindfulness Being present by focusing your attention on where you are and what you are doing

mudra Hand poses to seal in the energy of the breath

parallel Having the same direction

prana (PRAH-nah) Breath or life force

sage A wise person

Sanskrit One of the world's oldest languages that is spoken from teacher to student to pass on knowledge and teachings in the oral tradition of yoga

Sivananda (SI-vah-nan-dah) **yoga**
A type of yoga based on five points that are practiced daily: proper exercise, proper breathing, proper relaxation, proper diet, and positive thinking

supine Lying face up on the back of the body

torso Upper body—chest and trunk—of the human body

Vinyasa (vin-YAH-sah) **yoga** A type of yoga that flows through dancelike moves from one pose to the next, developed from Ashtanga yoga

viral Something that quickly becomes very popular or well known by being published on the Internet

yoga A system of physical poses and breathing exercises to unite mind and body

yogi A male who does yoga

yogini A female who does yoga